First World War
and Army of Occupation
War Diary
France, Belgium and Germany

58 DIVISION
174 Infantry Brigade
London Regiment
2/5 Battalion
24 January 1917 - 31 January 1918

WO95/3005/2

Published by

The Naval & Military Press Ltd

Unit 10 Ridgewood Industrial Park,

Uckfield, East Sussex,

TN22 5QE England

Tel: +44 (0) 1825 749494

www.naval-military-press.com

www.nmarchive.com

This diary has been reprinted in facsimile from the original. Any imperfections are inevitably reproduced and the quality may fall short of modern type and cartographic standards.

© Crown Copyright
Images reproduced by permission of The National Archives, London, England, 2015.

Contents

Document type	Place/Title	Date From	Date To
Heading	WO95/3005/2		
Heading	War Diary of 2/5th London Regt Vol 54		
War Diary	Southampton	24/01/1917	24/01/1917
War Diary	Havre	25/01/1917	26/01/1917
War Diary	Auxi-Le-Chateau	27/01/1917	27/01/1917
War Diary	Rougefay	28/01/1917	01/02/1917
War Diary	Fonquevillers	02/02/1917	05/02/1917
War Diary	Souastre	06/02/1917	08/02/1917
War Diary	Fonquevillers	09/02/1917	17/02/1917
War Diary	Souastre	18/02/1917	20/02/1917
War Diary	Ransart Sector C1 Sheet 51c S.E. W.12	25/02/1917	28/02/1917
War Diary	Humbercamp	01/03/1917	01/03/1917
War Diary	Ransart Section As Above	04/03/1917	05/03/1917
War Diary	Blairville Sheet 51c S.E. 4	06/03/1917	17/03/1917
War Diary	Bailleulval	18/03/1917	24/03/1917
War Diary	Boisleux-St-Marc	25/03/1917	27/03/1917
War Diary	Boisleux-Au-Mont	28/03/1917	28/03/1917
War Diary	Pommier	29/03/1917	29/03/1917
War Diary	Grouches	30/03/1917	01/04/1917
War Diary	Bouret	02/04/1917	02/04/1917
War Diary	Quoeux	04/04/1917	04/04/1917
War Diary	Mailly-Maillet	07/04/1917	07/04/1917
War Diary	Bihucourt	08/04/1917	25/04/1917
Heading	War Diary of 2/5th Bn Lon Regt From 26/4/17 To 24/5/17 Vol 5		
War Diary	Bihucourt	26/04/1917	14/05/1917
War Diary	Mory	15/05/1917	15/05/1917
War Diary	Ecoust-St-Mein	16/05/1917	17/05/1917
War Diary	Bullecourt	17/05/1917	18/05/1917
War Diary	Mory	20/05/1917	25/05/1917
War Diary	Longatte	26/05/1917	27/05/1917
War Diary	Ecoust	28/05/1917	30/05/1917
War Diary	Bullecourt	31/05/1917	03/06/1917
War Diary	Mory	04/06/1917	16/06/1917
War Diary	St Leger	16/06/1917	16/06/1917
War Diary	Croisilles Sector	17/06/1917	19/06/1917
War Diary	St Leger	20/06/1917	21/06/1917
War Diary	Courcelles	22/06/1917	30/06/1917
Heading	War Diary of 2/5th London Regt 1/7/17 To 31/7/17 Vol 7		
War Diary	Courcelles	01/07/1917	06/07/1917
War Diary	Bancourt	07/07/1917	07/07/1917
War Diary	Equancourt	08/07/1917	08/07/1917
War Diary	Beaucamp	09/07/1917	16/07/1917
War Diary	Ytres	19/07/1917	22/07/1917
War Diary	Trescault	23/07/1917	28/07/1917
War Diary	Ruyaulcourt	29/07/1917	29/07/1917
War Diary	Berneville	30/07/1917	24/08/1917
War Diary	Poperinghe	26/08/1917	26/08/1917
War Diary	Reigersburg	28/08/1917	31/08/1917

Heading	2/5 London Regt Sept 1917		
Heading	23 Div 68 69 70 Bdes		
War Diary	Reigersburg	01/09/1917	05/09/1917
War Diary	St Julien	08/09/1917	12/09/1917
War Diary	Dambre	13/09/1917	18/09/1917
War Diary	Reigersburg	19/09/1917	19/09/1917
War Diary	St Julien	20/09/1917	21/09/1917
War Diary	Reigersburg	22/09/1917	22/09/1917
War Diary	Brake Camp	23/09/1917	27/09/1917
War Diary	Licques	28/09/1917	30/09/1917
Miscellaneous	Report On Operations 20/9/17 2/5th Battn. London Regiment (L.R.B)		
Operation(al) Order(s)	Operation Order No. 23 3/6th BN The London Regiment	26/09/1917	26/09/1917
War Diary	Licques	01/10/1917	19/10/1917
War Diary	Poperinghe	20/10/1917	20/10/1917
War Diary	Seige Camp	24/10/1917	25/10/1917
War Diary	Canal Bank	26/10/1917	28/10/1917
War Diary	Kempton Park	29/10/1917	29/10/1917
War Diary	Poelcapelle	30/10/1917	31/10/1917
War Diary	Siege Camp	01/11/1917	08/11/1917
War Diary	Canal Bank	10/11/1917	10/11/1917
War Diary	Kempton Park	11/11/1917	12/11/1917
War Diary	Poelcapelle	13/11/1917	14/11/1917
War Diary	Kempton Park	15/11/1917	15/11/1917
War Diary	Canal Bank	16/11/1917	16/11/1917
War Diary	Siege Camp	17/11/1917	17/11/1917
War Diary	Herzeele	18/11/1917	25/11/1917
War Diary	Proven	26/11/1917	26/11/1917
War Diary	Seninghem	27/11/1917	27/11/1917
War Diary	Lottinghem	28/11/1917	07/12/1917
War Diary	Coulomby	08/12/1917	08/12/1917
War Diary	F Camp	09/12/1917	09/12/1917
War Diary	Dirty Bucket	10/12/1917	12/12/1917
War Diary	Huddlestone Camp	13/12/1917	07/01/1918
War Diary	Road Camp Proven (St Jan-Ter-Bietzen)	08/01/1918	18/01/1918
War Diary	Moreuil	19/01/1918	30/01/1918
War Diary	Berteaucourt	30/01/1918	30/01/1918
War Diary	Thennes	30/01/1918	31/01/1918
Miscellaneous			

WO 95/3005/2

144/58

WAR DIARY
OF
21st LONDON REGT.

Army Form C. 2118

WAR DIARY of 2/5th LONDON REGT. L.R.B.
or
INTELLIGENCE SUMMARY
(Erase heading not required.)

Place	Date 1917	Hour	Summary of Events and Information	Remarks and references to Appendices
Southampton	Jany 24		Battn left Sutton Veny by two trains, one at 9.30 am, the other at 10.20 am for Southampton. There split up into 3 parties for Embarkation: two parties reached Havre that night, but one party including Colonel & 450 all ranks put back when 10 miles out owing to bad weather. F.F.	
Havre	" 25		3rd Party put off again in same boat, reaching HAVRE at midnight. F.F.	
"	" 26		Whole Battalion left HAVRE rest camp at 5 p.m., Entraining at 7 p.m. F.F.	
Auxi-le-Chateau	" 27		Reached ABBEVILLE 4.45 p.m., and detrained at AUXI-LE-CHATEAU at 11 p.m. F.F.	
Rougefay	" 28		Arrived ROUGEFAY by road at 3 am, where battalion (less 1 company at BACHIMONT) was billeted F.F. Map LENS 3 BC $\frac{1}{100,000}$. F.F.	

LIEUTENANT-COLONEL,
COMMANDING
2/5TH (CITY OF LONDON) BATTN.
(LONDON RIFLE BRIGADE)

Army Form C. 2118

Vol. 2.

WAR DIARY of 2/5th London Regt. L.R.B.
or
INTELLIGENCE SUMMARY

(Erase heading not required.)

for month of Feby 1917

Instructions regarding War Diaries and Intelligence Summaries are contained in F.S. Regs., Part II. and the Staff Manual respectively. Title Pages will be prepared in manuscript.

Place	Date	Hour	Summary of Events and Information	Remarks and references to Appendices
ROUGEFAY	Feby 1	6 am	Transport left ROUGEFAY for HENU arriving at 5 p.m.	
		10 am	Battalion left ROUGEFAY by motor-bus & lorry, detraining at SOUASTRE at 3.30 p.m. Major P.D. Johnson left behind sick, & evacuated to hospital at DOULLENS 2/Lieut; J.F. Legg left at ROUGEFAY in charge of 9 sick. Tea at Autheux. SOUASTRE, then Battalion (less transport at HENU and Nos 15 & 16 Platoons at SOUASTRE) marched to FONQUEVILLERS & went into trenches as follows:— H.Q., A & B Coes to X1 Sector intermingled with 6th Notts & Derby, C & D Coes (the latter less 2 platoons) to X2 Sector intermingled with 8th Notts & Derby. 10 to 20 degrees of frost, snow on ground. N.E. wind, bright moon good visibility. Enemy patrol approached our line at 11 am, driven off by Lewis Gun & Rifle fire	77.
FONQUEVILLERS	Feby 2	4 p.m.	H.Q. moved at 4 p.m. with H.Q. 6th Notts. Derby from the trenches to the Brasserie, FONQUEVILLERS 1 other rank: wounded by shell fire. Germans sent out small bombing party, chokened by our fire. Two killed bodies Nos 15 & 16 platoons joined their Company in the trenches retrieved & establishd that Reserve Guards opposite us Still hard frost, with N.E. wind, & clear.	77.
"	Feby 3	5.30 pm	A & B Coes out of trenches to billets at SOUASTRE, C & D to billets at FONQUEVILLERS	
		9.30 pm	Heavy Draught Horse killed by shrapnel on FONQUEVILLERS - SOUASTRE Road while taking down cooker. Hard frost continues, same conditions.	77.
"	Feby 4	5.30 pm	A & B Coes went into X2 Sector by platoons, relieving part of 8th Notts & Derby, who were afterwards totally relieved by 7th Notts & Derby. C & D Coes went into X1 Sector by platoons, relieving part of 6th Notts & Derby, who were afterwards totally relieved by 5th Notts & Derby. Hard frost continues, with N.E. wind & clear. Patrols active by night, though hindered by bright moon, & very little work able to be done in trenches owing to frozen ground.	77.
"	Feby 5	5 p.m.	All 4 Companies remained in same sectors, but working as separate Companies. H.Q. moved to SOUASTRE. Capt: J.M. Naylor slightly wounded in leg by sniper, & evacuated to Cas: Clearing Station.	77.

Army Form C. 2118

WAR DIARY of 2/5 London L.R.B.
INTELLIGENCE SUMMARY
(Erase heading not required.)

Instructions regarding War Diaries and Intelligence Summaries are contained in F.S. Regs., Part II. and the Staff Manual respectively. Title Pages will be prepared in manuscript.

Place	Date	Hour	Summary of Events and Information for Feby 1917	Remarks and references to Appendices
SOUASTRE	Feby 6	5.30 p.m.	All 4 Companies out of trenches to Divisional Reserve at SOUASTRE. Intensely cold weather continues, wind N.E.	J.J.
"	7		Weather same. J.J. Capt G. Whitaker to 3rd Army Course at AUXI-LE-CHATEAU. J.J.	
"	8		Battalion relieved 5th Sherwood Foresters & took over XI Sector at FONQUEVILLERS, relief being completed by 7.40 p.m. Cold weather continues, wind N.E. J.J. Major R.D. Johnson rejoined from hospital. J.J.	
FONQUEVILLERS	9		Intermittent Shelling on both sides day & night, otherwise situation quiet. Cold, wind N.E. J.J. 2/Lieut G.F. Legg rejoined. J.J.	
"	10		ditto — Cold; clouded over during night, wind N.E. J.J.	
"	11		ditto — our snipers active. Slightly warmer — wind N.E. J.J.	
"	12		Battalion relieved by 5th Sherwood Foresters, relief completed by 9 p.m. Returned to SOUASTRE to Divisional Reserve. One casualty other ranks, slight wound in face by shell splinter. J.J.	
"	15		Battalion relieved 5th Sherwood Foresters & took over XI Sector at FONQUEVILLERS, relief being completed by 9 p.m. 50 men to GRENAS at 2 p.m. to form Brigade Pioneer Coy. J.J.	
"	16		Enemy shelled FONQUEVILLERS heavily at 6.30 p.m. & 8.30 p.m., mostly Trench Mortars, for periods of about 20 mins = an artillery retaliated. One casualty other ranks wounded. Wind to S. thaw set in afternoon. 2/Lieut W.H. Mitchell to GRENAS to take charge of our 50 men for Brigade Pioneer Coy. J.J.	
"	17		Enemy shelled FONQUEVILLERS heavily at 1 a.m. & 3.30 a.m., mostly Trench Mortars, for period of about 20 mins = our artillery retaliated. Battalion relieved by 5th Sherwood Foresters, relief completed by 9 p.m. Returned to SOUASTRE to Divisional Reserve. 1 Casualty accidentally wounded other ranks. Wind S. warmer. J.J.	
SOUASTRE	18		2/Lieut R. Cope with 4 other ranks to wireless course at PAS. J.J.	
"	20		2/Lieut C.F. Joyce with party to BAILLEULMONT as L.T.M. Reserve Battery. J.J. Battalion moved by road to BAILLEULMONT, leaving SOUASTRE by platoons commencing at 5 a.m. J.J. Battalion relieved 27th London in sector C1, W11+12 Sheet 51 C.S.E., relief completed by 3.30 p.m. J.J.	G.H.Q. to O/L R/H London to 2/5[?]

Army Form C. 2118

WAR DIARY of 2/5th London Regt. L.R.B.

INTELLIGENCE SUMMARY

(Erase heading not required.)

Instructions regarding War Diaries and Intelligence Summaries are contained in F.S. Regs., Part II. and the Staff Manual respectively. Title Pages will be prepared in manuscript.

JFL 3

Place	Date 1917	Hour	Summary of Events and Information	Remarks and references to Appendices
RANSART SECTOR C1 Sheet 51C S.E. W.12.	Feb 25		Following Message received 12.45 am:– "Indications point to enemy having retired along front of 5th Corps. Patrols are being sent out towards SERRE, PUISIEUX and GOMMECOURT; be ready to send out patrols and to move on receipt of further orders; patrols to be sent out should be a platoon strong with a Lewis Gun + reconnoitre the German front line". Battalion stood to till 10 am ready to advance. Patrols sent out at night discovered that Germans still in front of our line. 2/Lieut Finlayson to Sharpshooters course at AUXI–LE–CHAPEAU. 2/Lieut Cope returned from Wireless Course. 77.	
	" 26		1 other rank killed by Sharpnel. 77.	
	" 28		Relieved by 2/7th Londons : relief complete by 12 noon. Battalion went into Divisional Reserve at HUMBERCAMP. 77.	
HUMBERCAMP	March 1		2/Lieut: C.F. Joyce + party returned from L.T.M. Battery. 77.	
Ransart Sector as above	" 4		Relieved 2/7th Londons : relief complete by 1 pm. 1 other rank killed, 1 wounded by shell fire 77, 2/Lieut J.F. Legg to anti-aircraft Lewis Gun Course 77.	
	" 5		1 other rank wounded shell fire. 77.	
BLAIRVILLE Sheet 51C S.E. 4.	" 6		Battalion extended to right (south), taking up fresh positions from W.18.a.30.85 to W.23.c.80.50.; one company + two platoons at BAILLEULVAL, two platoons on Ridge Road, + two companies by platoons in detached posts along the line – H.Q. at W.17.d.15.35; 2/5 took over part of our left, + we relieved part of 2/7 London on our right. 77. Companies relieve every 6 days. 2/Lt F.R.H. Newington (2o. London) joined. 2/Lt V.A. Finlayson & J.F. Legg returned from Courses 77.	
	" 11		Batt H.Q. moved back to BAILLEULVAL – 1 other rank killed, 1 wounded, 1 shell shock – 77.	
	" 12		2/Lt E.W. Fuller to L.G. Course, Brigade School, HUMBERCAMP. 77.	
	" 13		1 other rank killed. 77.	
	" 14		2/Lt A.S. Wimble to Staff Instructional Course (17th Inf. Bgde.) 77.	
	" 15		2/Lt A.H. Scholfield (19th London) joined, Lieut G. Whitaker returned from Course – Patrols	
	" 17		discovered enemy had retired from our front. 77.	

WAR DIARY 2/5 London, LRB. Army Form C. 2118

or

INTELLIGENCE SUMMARY

(Erase heading not required.)

Place	Date 1917	Hour	Summary of Events and Information	Remarks and references to Appendices
BAILLEULVAL	Mch 18		Following 7 officers & 15 O.R joined from base :- 2/Lts H.C.Linnott, C.G.Brentford, W.E.Green, Q.M.Pilcher, B.R.Power, H.W.Sampson, D.T.Ward. Battalion into Divisional Reserve at BAILLEULVAL 7.7.	
	"	20	2/Lieut H.W.Sampson to Hospital 7.7.	
	"	21	2/Lieut F.W.Fuller rejoined from Bgde L.G. Course. Battalion road making at BELLACOURT under R.E. Supervision. Capt H.S.Palmer RAMC to Sanitary Course at ST POL 7.7.	
	"	22	Battalion moved S. to POMMIER - Draft of 87 men joined. 7.7.	
	"	23	Battalion moved to BOISLEUX - AU MONT, relieving 2/1 Londons in support of battalion in the new line 7.7.	
	"	24	Battalion relieved 2/2 Londons in the line, taking up an outpost line from BOIRY - BECQUERELLES to BOYELLES, with 2 Companies in the line, 2 Companies in support (one at BOISLEUX - ST-MARC, the other in cutting at S18a and S18c). Battn H.Q. being at S11d.4.3. 7.7.	

M.Marshall Lt.
2/5 London Regt.
LRB

Army Form C. 2118

WAR DIARY of 2/5 LONDON, L.R.B.
or
INTELLIGENCE SUMMARY
(Erase heading not required.)

Vol 4

Instructions regarding War Diaries and Intelligence Summaries are contained in F.S. Regs, Part II. and the Staff Manual respectively. Title Pages will be prepared in manuscript.

Place	Date 1917	Hour	Summary of Events and Information	Remarks and references to Appendices
BOISLEUX-ST-MARC	March 25	1 p.m.	Prisoner of 99th Regiment captured by party of Intelligence Section outside BOIRY BECQUERELLES at 1 p.m. 2/Lieut G.F. Trenow rejoined, Lieut C.H. Jones to 3rd Army School, AUXI-LE-CHATEAU. Lieut G. Shillito (19th London) joined. 1 other rank wounded. 7.7.	
"	" 27		1 other rank killed; 1 O.R. wounded-shell shock. Batt. relieved to BOISLEUX-AUMONT, being relieved by 12th Northumberland Fusiliers. 7.7.	
BOISLEUX AU-MONT	" 28		Batt. relieved by 10th Yorks, returning to POMMIER 7.7.	
POMMIER	" 29		Batt. marched to Hut Camp near GROUCHES 7.7.	
GROUCHES	" 30		2/Lieut. G.H. Ticehurst joined 7.7.	
"	April 1		Batt. marched to Billets at BOURET-SUR-CANCHE. 7.7.	
BOURET	" 2		Batt. marched to Billets at QUOEUX, HAUT-MAISNIL & HARAVESNES, Batt. H.Q. at QUOEUX. 7.7.	
QUOEUX	" 4		Batt. moved by bus to MAILLY-MAILLET into billets, transport by road taking 2 days over journey 7.7. Major G. Harvest to Hospital 7.7.	
MAILLY-MAILLET	" 7		Batt. marched to canvas & bivouac camp ½ mile E of BIHUCOURT (S. of ACHIET-LE-GRAND) 7.7. & repairing	
BIHUCOURT	" 8-14		Batt. at work all day road-making at ERVILLERS and MORY 7.7.	
"	" 14		One other rank wounded, German trip wire bomb 7.7.	
"	" 10		Major G. Harvest returned to duty from Hospital 7.7.	
"	" 12		Major G. Harvest to hospital 7.7.	
"	" 12-17		Batt. road repairing round MORY 7.7.	
"	" 18		Batt. training by Companies & platoons 7.7.	

1875 Wt. W593/826 1,000,000 4/15 J.B.C. & A. A.D.S.S./Forms/C. 2118.

Army Form C. 2118

WAR DIARY of 2/5 London Regt LRB
or
INTELLIGENCE SUMMARY
(Erase heading not required.)

Instructions regarding War Diaries and Intelligence Summaries are contained in F. S. Regs., Part II. and the Staff Manual respectively. Title Pages will be prepared in manuscript.

Place	Date 1917	Hour	Summary of Events and Information	Remarks and references to Appendices
BIHUCOURT	April	19-21	Road repairing at NOREUIL & work under R.E.s. 7.7.	
"	"	21	Capt E.D. Johnson to permanent base duty - unfit 7.7.	
"	"	22	Training by Companies & Platoons 7.7.	
"	"	23	Work under R.E.s. Lt Col P.D. Stewart (3rd Dragoon Guards) assumed command of Battalion vice Lt Col G.R. Tod returned to England on account of age 7.7.	
"	"	24	2 Coys Training, 2 Road Work 7.7.	
"	"	25	do do 2/Lieut W.H. Mitchell & 50 O.R. returned to duty with Battalion from Pioneer Coy, R.E. 2/Lieut A.H. Scholefield returned to duty from Div. Salvage Co. 7.7.	

J Stewart Lt Col
Bihucourt 2/5 London Regt
Comg.

17/38

NB 5

CONFIDENTIAL
✶✶✶✶✶✶✶✶✶✶✶✶

WAR DIARY

OF

2/5th Dn Leic Regt

From 26/4/17
To 24/5/17

Army Form C. 2118.

WAR DIARY of 2/5 London, LRB
INTELLIGENCE SUMMARY.

(Erase heading not required.)

Instructions regarding War Diaries and Intelligence Summaries are contained in F.S. Regs., Part II and the Staff Manual respectively. Title pages will be prepared in manuscript.

Place	Hour, Date, 1917	Summary of Events and Information	Remarks and references to Appendices
BIHUCOURT	April 26-30	Working parties under R.E. day & night. Training at all odd hours possible 7.7.	
	29	Lieut C.H. Jones returned from course at AUXI-LE-CHATEAU 7.7.	
	30	Capt C. Furze proceeded on leave to England 7.7.	
	May 1-2	Working parties under R.E. 7.7.	
	2	2/Lieut C.F. Joyce & O.R. to L.T.M. Course, VALHEUREUX 7.7.	
	3	Lieut E.W. Fuller proceeded to VAUCHELLES for instruction	
		V Corps School 7.7.	
	3-4	Working parties under R.E. 7.7.	
	6	Capt T.L. Otto to Signalling School CONTAY 7.7.	
	5-8	Battalion Training 7.7.	
	9	2/Lieut A.M. Pilcher & O.R. to 5th Corps School, VAUCHELLES 7.7.	
		Battalion Training 7.7.	
	10	— do — Capt G.C. Kitching on leave to England 7.7.	
	11	Brigade Training 7.7.	
	12	Working parties & Coy Training — 2/Lt D.T. Ward & party to Summer Rest Camp, ST VALERY SUR SOMME 7.7.	
	13	Working parties & Coy Training 7.7.	
	14	Battalion left camp near BIHUCOURT, and took over camp from 2nd Warwicks near MORY 7.7.	

Army Form C. 2118.

WAR DIARY of 2/5 London, LRB
INTELLIGENCE SUMMARY.
(Erase heading not required.)

Instructions regarding War Diaries and Intelligence Summaries are contained in F.S. Regs., Part II. and the Staff Manual respectively. Title pages will be prepared in manuscript.

Hour, Date, Place		Summary of Events and Information	Remarks and references to Appendices
MORY	May 15 1917	Lieut V.E.O. Welch on leave to England – 2/Lieut G.H. Ticehurst to L.G. Course, ETAPLES. Battalion moved out at 5 a.m. and lay out in the fields between MORY and ECOUST, ready to reinforce – H.Q. and 2 Coys returned to camp at 10.30 a.m. other 2 Coys at 4 p.m. Battalion moved up into line at 8 p.m., "A" Coy to railway line S.W. of BULLECOURT at U.27.C., H.Q. & "B" Coy in support at ECOUST ST MEIN, "C" & "D" Coys in reserve between MORY & ECOUST 7.7.	
ECOUST ST MEIN	" 16	H.Q. and "B" Coy moved up to railway embankment at 11 a.m. to prepare for attack on BULLECOURT at 2 p.m.; attack cancelled at 1 p.m.; H.Q. & "A" Coy returned to ECOUST, "B" Coy remaining in line. "C" & "D" Coys came up to ECOUST at 7 p.m. in preparation for attack on BULLECOURT 7.7.	
"	" 17	BULLECOURT (H. section part of the village being held by 2/8th London) attacked by the battalion at zero+2', preceded by a hurricane barrage on trenches S.W. of village at zero (2 a.m.). Battalion attacked on a double coy frontage of 400 yards from U.27.d.4.9. to U.27.a.8.8. being formed up ready for the assault, about 300 yards from the trenches at zero – 1 hour. "A" on right, "B" on left and 2 platoons of "C" on left specially detailed to take strong points at U.27.b-1.8. 2 Platoons of "C" in support on railway line, "D" Coy in reserve. The #1 Platoon of "C" detailed to relieve 2 Platoons of "B" on railway line failed to reach the rendezvous in time owing to darkness, so that their place in the Second wave on the left was taken by 1 Platoon of "C" Coy finally leaving 2 Platoons of "D" & 1 of "C" in support. 1st Objective of 2 Coys – line of trenches between the two roads on S.W. outskirts of village. 2nd Objective – Road from U.27.b.7.5.45. to U.27.b.15.85. 7.7. cont'd	

WAR DIARY of 2/5 London LRB
or
INTELLIGENCE SUMMARY.

(Erase heading not required.)

Army Form C. 2118.

Hour, Date, Place		Summary of Events and Information	Remarks and references to Appendices
BULLECOURT	May 17 Cont'd	All objectives taken = a number of Germans killed, 23 captured. In the evening the Battalion took over whole of the village, relieving the 2/8th on right, our line being from U 22 c 9.8. to U 27/6 2.8. Batt: H.Q. at U 28 a 40.15.	
"	18	Relieved by 2/6th at nightfall, whole battalion returning to camp at MORY. Total casualties in operation May 17/18 as follows :— 2/Lieut: A.H. Scholefield killed Capt: F.P. Barry, Lieut: C. Shillito 2/Lieut F.R.H. Newington wounded 2/Lieut V.A. Finlayson fell down well, rescued completely exhausted after 6 hours. 11 O.R. killed, 33 wounded.	
MORY	20	Lieut H.G. Wilkinson to Genl Course at TOUTENCOURT Capt & Adjt F. Furg on leave to England. Capt: C.E. Johnston arrived for duty. All Companies on working parties at night ECOUST – BULLECOURT	
"	21	Coys resting. Later – at work repairing camp on higher ground.	
"	23	raining.	
"	24	Raining. At night see Battalion on working parties ECOUST. 2/Lt H.W. Sampson joined from HUTHUSH? are working party ECOUST at night	

174 58

WAR DIARY of 2/5 LONDON REGT (L.R.B.)
INTELLIGENCE SUMMARY.

Army Form C. 2118.

Vol 6

Hour, Date, Place 1917	Summary of Events and Information	Remarks and references to Appendices
MORY May 25	Working Parties etc – J.J.	
LONGATTE " 26	Moved up into support, relieving 2/8th London in right sub-sector. Battn. H.Q. on LONGATTE - NOREUIL Road. 2/Lieut G.H.Ticehurst returned from L.G.Course. J.J. 1 O.R. Killed, 1 O.R. wounded.	
" 27	3 O.R. wounded. 2/Lt W.E.Green to Stokes Mortar School, VAUCHELLES. 2/Lieut D.T.Wand returned from Rest Camp. J.J.	
ECOUST " 28	Battn. H.Q. moved to ECOUST-ST-MEIN, Coys remaining as before. 3 O.R. wounded. J.J.	
" 29	Lieut V.E.O. Welch returned from leave. 2/Lieut F.Williamson reported for duty. J.J.	
" 30	Battn. relieved 2/8th London in front line, right sub-sector. E of BULLECOURT, Battn. H.Q. at Railway Embankment, C.4.b. Capt. T.L.Forbes proceeded on leave. 2 O.R. wounded. J.J.	
BULLECOURT " 31	Nil	
June 1	8 O.R. Wounded. J.J.	
" 2	2/Lieuts F.E.Pattison & J.F.Legg and 13 O.R. wounded J.J.	
" 3	Battn. relieved by 2/11th London, returned to MORY. 4 O.R. wounded. 2/Lieut B.R.Power to L.G.Course, LE TOUQUET. Capt.-Adjt. F.Furze returned from leave. J.J.	
MORY " 4	Capt. C.E. Johnston proceeded on leave. 6 O.R. wounded at battn. by shell fire. J.J.	A Coy Sgt Potter C.G. 300912 Hoot Foster G.E. 301491 Rfn Wright T.F. 300417 Sgt Busher J.A. 362,508 Rfn Ewins V.B. } Military Medal J.J.

WAR DIARY of 2/5 London (LRB)
or INTELLIGENCE SUMMARY.

(Erase heading not required.)

Army Form C. 2118.

Instructions regarding War Diaries and Intelligence Summaries are contained in F.S. Regs., Part II. and the Staff Manual respectively. Title pages will be prepared in manuscript.

Hour, Date, Place	1917	Summary of Events and Information	Remarks and references to Appendices
MORY	June 5	1 O.R. wounded shell in Camp - Training & Working Parties F.7.	
	" 6	Training & Working Parties - Reinforcing draft of 4 men arrived F.7.	
	" 7-10	Training & Working Parties F.7.	
	" 9	2/Lieuts W.E. Green & A.M. Pilcher returned from course F.7.	
	" 10	2/Lieuts G.F. Trenow & C.F. Joyce with 4 Other Ranks to 5th Army Sniping Course. F.7. Steamer Rest Camp, VALERY-SUR-SOMME. Lieut: C.H. Jones to 5th Army Sniping Course, VADENCOURT 2/Lieut: G.H. Ticehurst to Hospital, sick. F.7.	
	" 11	Training & Working Parties. Capt: T.L. Forbes returned from leave. Lieut G.L. Harvest } Major 2/Lieut F.P. Barry } Military 300640 Sgt Howells F.9. "C" Coy F.7. " G.F. Trenow } Cross Military Medal F.7.	
	" 12/13	Training & Working Parties. F.7.	
	" 14	Camp at B.28.C. (except Transport, Q.M. Stores & Details) taken over by 2/12th Ldn., the Batt'n moving to B.27.a (½ a mile away to the west) & taking over from 8th Devons at 9 p.m. F.7.	
	" 15	Moved from camp ½ mile S.W. to camp ½ mile N.W. of MORY at B.15.b, taking over camp from 2/2nd Ldn at 9 p.m. 2/Lt M.C.K. McKenzie Smith (18th London) joined for duty. F.7.	
	" 16	Orders received at 2 a.m. to move to ST LEGER at 6 a.m. to be ready to support 173rd Brigade, who had temporarily lost part of Hindenburg line E. of CROISILLES (gained previous day) by a counter attack. Batt'n moved on again from ST LEGER at 9 p.m. and took over HINDENBURG front line from details of 173rd Bgde from U.20.b.4.3 to U.14.c.2.9. Lieut G. Whittaker went on leave. Capt E.E. Johnston returned from leave F.7.	
ST LEGER			

Army Form C. 2118.

WAR DIARY of 2/5 London (LRB)
or
INTELLIGENCE SUMMARY.
(Erase heading not required.)

Instructions regarding War Diaries and Intelligence Summaries are contained in F.S. Regs., Part II. and the Staff Manual respectively. Title pages will be prepared in manuscript.

Place	Hour, Date	Summary of Events and Information	Remarks and references to Appendices
CROISILLES Sector	June 17 1917	Relief complete by 3 am. The following platoons did not relieve, but went forward as strong patrols to enter HINDENBURG support line if possible and reinforce some elements of 173rd Brigade who possibly might still be holding out there. 2 Platoons of "D" Coy under Capt. T.L. Forbes and 2/Lt W.E. Green went forward on left; received with heavy fire and forced to return. 1 Platoon of "B" Coy under 2/Lt C.G. Brentford and 1 of "D" Coy, the whole under Lieut. V.E.O. Welch went forward together on right; lost their way, and finally discovered at 11 p.m. in shell holes in rear of our front line. "C" Coy on right pushed forward a platoon to a MEBUS between the lines which they consolidated & held during the tour, handing over on relief. Capt. T.L. Forbes, Lieut. V.E.O. Welch & 2/Lieut. C.G. Brentford wounded. 11 O.R. Killed. 18 wounded, 3 wounded at duty. 2/Lieut. F. Williamson to General Course, 2/Lt H.W. Sampson to Bombing Course, VAUCHELLES 7.7.	
	18	2/Lts L. Forbes, H.C. Liddle & M.C.K. McKenzie-Smith wounded. 8 O.R. Killed, 33 wounded, 5 wounded at duty. Capt. F.L. Otter rejoined from Signalling Course.	7.7.
	19	Lieut. G.L. Harvest M.C. wounded (died of wounds 20th). 9 O.R. Killed, 14 wounded, 1 wounded at duty. Capt. F.L. Otter took over command of "B" Coy. Relieved by 2/7th Londons Battn. returning to ST LEGER 7.7. Commencing at 9.30 pm.	

Army Form C. 2118.

WAR DIARY of 2/5 Ldn (L.R.B.)
of
INTELLIGENCE SUMMARY.
(Erase heading not required.)

Instructions regarding War Diaries and Intelligence Summaries are contained in F.S. Regs., Part II and the Staff Manual respectively. Title pages will be prepared in manuscript.

Hour, Date, Place	1917	Summary of Events and Information	Remarks and references to Appendices
ST LEGER	June 20	Relief complete by 3 am / Batt⁹ moved to COURCELLES 77	
	21	Commencing 6 p.m. being relieved at ST LEGER by 1st South Staffords. Detail Camp also moved from MORY. Transport - 2/Lt B.R. Power returned from L.G. Course, LE TOUQUET. 2/Lts W.D. Jenkins, L.G. Hammerton + G.R. Reeve joined for duty. 77	
COURCELLES	22	Training & Reorganisation & Re equipment. 77	
"	23	Training. Lt Col P.D. Stewart proceeded on leave. Lieut: H.G. Watkinson returned from Course at TOUTENCOURT 77. 1 O.R. wounded, self inflicted accidentally 77.	
"	24	2/Lieuts H.C. Dutton (18th London) and L. Smetham joined for duty. Lieut: C.H. Jones rejoined from Snipers Course. 2/Lieuts G.F. Trenow M.C. & C.F. Joyce rejoined from Rest Camp. 77. Training & Working Parties. Draft of 24 O.R. joined. 77.	
"	25	—do— 2/Lt R. Cope proceeded on leave. 77	
"	26	Lieut: C.H. Jones to Hospital sick. 77.	
"	28	Capt F.L. Otter to 2 days course with R.F.C. near COURCELLES on Signalling to Contact aeroplanes. Lieut: G.H. Ticehurst rejoined from Hospital 77.	
"	29	Lieut: G. Whitaker rejoined from leave 77.	
"	30	Capt: C. Furze proceeded to HAVRE for a 2 months tour of duty as Instructor for Training of Reinforcements.	

WAR DIARY Vol 7

2/15th London Regt.
1/4/17 to 31/12/17

WAR DIARY of 2/5 London Regt. (L.R.B.)

INTELLIGENCE SUMMARY.

(Erase heading not required.)

Army Form C. 2118.

Instructions regarding War Diaries and Intelligence Summaries are contained in F.S. Regs., Part II and the Staff Manual respectively. Title pages will be prepared in manuscript.

Place	Hour, Date.	Summary of Events and Information	Remarks and references to Appendices
COURCELLES	July 1 1917	2/Lt H.W. Sampson rejoined from Bombing Course. VAUCHELLES. 2/Lt W.H.L. Mitchell proceeded on leave. J.J.	
"	3	2/Lt G.F. Trenow M.C. to General Course 5th Army School, TOUTENCOURT. Brigade Transport Sports in afternoon. J.J.	
"	4	Lieut. C.H. Jones rejoined from Hospital. Officer Commanding, Adjutant & 4 Coy Commanders proceeded by bus to view new line from BEAUCAMPS to VILLERS PLOUICH, returning same night. J.J.	
"	5	Major C.E. Johnston proceeded to England to Senior Officers Course, ALDERSHOT. J.J.	
"	6	Lt Col. P.D. Stewart rejoined from leave. Battalion moved at 3 pm to BANCOURT, all 58th Division moving to New area, arrived Camp 6 pm J.J.	
BANCOURT	" 7	Left BANCOURT 2.45 pm, reached camp at EQUANCOURT at 6.45 pm. Transport & Q.M. Stores to Permanent Camp ½ mile N of FINS J.J.	
EQUANCOURT	" 8	Left EQUANCOURT at 8 pm & proceeded up into the line, taking over a two Battalion frontage from the 2/5 & 2/8 Notts & Derby from VILLERS PLOUICH to BEAUCAMP, the front line being about a mile N of these two villages – all Companies in the line, finding their own supports. Battn H.Q. in sunken road between the two villages. J.J.	
BEAUCAMP	" 9	Relief complete by 2.25 am. J.J.	
"	10	Two small parties of enemy attempted raid at 3 am, one on our left front, one on right front of battalion on our left (2/7 London). Both driven off before reaching trenches. Casualties unknown – 2/Lt R. Cope rejoined from leave. 1 O.R. killed, 5 O.R. wounded J.J.	Postponed

WAR DIARY of 2/5 London Regt (L.R.B.)

INTELLIGENCE SUMMARY.

(Erase heading not required.)

Army Form C. 2118.

Hour, Date, Place		Summary of Events and Information	Remarks and references to Appendices
BEAUCAMP	1917 July 11	Casualties 1 O.R. Killed 7.7. Capt. Rev. T. Vernon Smith awarded Military Cross 7.7.	
"	12	2/Lt W.D. Jenkins took over duties of Town Major, NEUVILLE. 7.7.	
"	13	2 O.R. killed 7.7.	
"	15	2/Lt W.H.L. Mitchell returned from leave – 2/Lt D.T. Ward proceeded to Musketry Course, WARLOY 7.7.	
"	16	Relieved by 2/3rd London, relief complete by 7 p.m. Battalion returned to Divisional Reserve at YTRES, about 5 miles by cross country light railway – while Battalion was in the line, a strong patrol of about 30 O.R. went out every night, but did not come in contact with the enemy at all 7.7.	
YTRES	19	2/Lt W.D. Jenkins returned from duty as Town Major 7.7. Capt. Rev. T. Vernon Smith proc. to Hospital, sick 7.9. Major E.C. Hill-Whitson, the Royal Scots, from 14th Battn Argyll & Sutherland Highlanders joined for duty, as 2nd in Command.	
"	20	2/Lt B.R. Power to R.F.C. LEALVILLERS for course of recognition of and firing at aircraft in connection with the Lewis Gun. 2/Lieuts. E.S. Higham, A.P. Sharman, J.S. Godward and R. Bronner joined <s>from duty</s> for duty 7.7.	
"	21	Capt. H.S. Palmer proceeded on leave to England. Lieut. W.H. Oxton joined as Medical Officer in place of Capt. Palmer whilst on leave. Lieut. F. Williamson rejoined from 5 Corps Course, VAUCHELLES 7.7.	
"	17/22	Training & Reorganisation at YTRES 7.7.	

Army Form C. 2118.

WAR DIARY of 2/5 London Regt. L.R.B.

INTELLIGENCE SUMMARY.
(Erase heading not required.)

Instructions regarding War Diaries and Intelligence Summaries are contained in F.S. Regs., Part II. and the Staff Manual respectively. Title pages will be prepared in manuscript.

Place	Hour, Date	Summary of Events and Information	Remarks and references to Appendices
	1917		
TRESCAULT	July 23	Relieved 2/6th London in the line travelling up by light railway: relief complete by 5:30 pm. Line approximately from BEAUCAMP to TRESCAULT, E. of HAVRINCOURT WOOD & 2 Coys in line, 1 in Support, 1 in Reserve near Batt⁻ H.Q. at Q10d 4.9. ½ mile NE of HAVRINCOURT WOOD.	
		80 NCOs came with 4 officers at NEUVILLE for training: Remainder (Transport Q.M. Stores etc.) to camp ½ mile N of FINS.	
	25	2/Lt B.R. Power rejoined from Course at LEALVILLERS 7.7.	
		Lt. C.H. Jones (for Bgde H.Q.) 2/Lt B.R. Power & 1 NCO proceeded to new Divisional Area as advanced billeting party.	
		2 Other ranks wounded	
		Draft 34 other ranks from 3rd Batt⁻ arrived 7.7.	
	26	Capt: Rev: E.M. Winter joined for duty 7.7.	
	27	2/Lt G.H. Ticehurst to G.H.Q. Lewis Gun Course, LE TOUQUET. 7.7.	
	28	Relieved by 1st S. African Regt: relief complete by 5.30 pm. Whole Battalion to Camp at RUYAULCOURT. 7.7.	
RUYAULCOURT	29	Left RUYAULCOURT at 7 pm by bus to BAPAUME, where batt⁻ entrained 7.7.	
BERNEVILLE	30	Arrived BEAUMETZ 2.30 am, detrained, marched to Camp at BERNEVILLE 7.7.	
	31	Following officers joined for duty :- 2/Lt J.W. Carrington, W.G. Grench and E.J.B. Miskin (all of the 19th London); and 2/Lt A.C. Young of this regiment. 7.7.	
		Draft of 61 other ranks joined 7.7.	

WAR DIARY of 2/5 London Regt (LRB)

INTELLIGENCE SUMMARY

Army Form C. 2118.

(Erase heading not required.)

Instructions regarding War Diaries and Intelligence Summaries are contained in F.S. Regs., Part II and the Staff Manual respectively. Title pages will be prepared in manuscript.

Hour, Date, Place	Summary of Events and Information	Remarks and references to Appendices
BERNEVILLE Aug 1 1917	2/Lt C.G. Hummerston to Hospital.	
	2/Lt C.F. Joyce to 174th L.T.M Battery 77.	
Aug 3	Mr W.O Jenkin to 2nd Convalescence	
	Capt. ? ? Wise resigns appointment of Adjutant	
	2/Lt R. Cope acting adjutant	
	Capt. ? ? Wise takes over command of D Coy until	
	Capt. Wickham returns from leave (2 Lieut in command). Capt. Wickham sent to	
	Infantry school 3? Army to command a company. RC	
4	2/Lt D.T. Ward returns from musketry course	
	WARLOY.	
	Lt H.G. Wickham goes on leave	RC
5	2/Lt G.H. Meekum returns from Lewis Gun Course	
	LE TOUQUET	RC
	2/Lt G.H. Hamer (19 London) joins for duty and	
	then from RC	
7	'C' Coy left for LIGNY ST FLOCHEL for training at	
	3rd Army Infantry School	RC
8	2/Lt G.F. Heron MC returns from infantry course	
	TOUTENCOURT RC	
9	2/Lt L.S. Owen (19 London) joins for duty. RC	
	2/Lt H.G. Ireland (19 London) joins for duty RC	
11	2/Lt W.E. Green to musketry Camp WARLOY RC	
12	2/Lt L. Smithers to 3rd Army Infantry School	
	AUXI-LE-CHATEAU RC	
	2/Lt L.G. Hummerston reported from 2nd Ambulance RC	P. Stewart

WAR DIARY of 2/5 London Regt. (L.R.B.)

INTELLIGENCE SUMMARY

Army Form C. 2118

(Erase heading not required.)

Place	Date AUG	Hour	Summary of Events and Information	Remarks and references to Appendices
BERNÉVILLE	13		"C" Coy returned from LIGNY ST FLOCHEL R.E.	
	15		Capt E.G. Moore and Hon. M. and Q. his H.J. Kent go on leave R.E.	
	20		Lts G Whitaker and H.S. Wellmann assume acting rank of Captain under Auth GRO 2494 R.E.	
	22		Lt Trucott returns from leave R.E.	
	24		The Battalion entrained at ARRAS at 9.54 am and travelled by train to GODWAERSVELDE, detrained and marched to POPERINGHE. Arrived 8 p.m. and billeted in the town R.E.	
POPERINGHE	26		Capts. J. Twigg, Otto Kieling, 7/Lt Wellmann Ziekum, Stammers, Mitchell and Sanderson to a 3 day course at XVIII Corps School VOLCKERINCKHOVE	
			2/Lt R.Brunner to 4 weeks course at do. R.E.	
			2/Lt H.C. Dutton returned from course in musketry at G.H.Q. R.E.	
REIGERS-BURG	28		Battalion mvd reserve at REIGERSBURG about 1 mile N.W. of YPRES on rupture battle front of 5 Main and 108 other ranks who proceeded to Divl Noton at HOUTKERQUE. R.E.	
"	29		7/Lt W.R. Green returned from WARLOY musketry court. R.E.	
"	30		2/Lt J.S. Crockard proceeded to reinf. from Lahore VOLCKERINCKHOVE R.E.	
"	31			

D.S. Stewart
LIEUTENANT-COLONEL
COMMANDING
2/5th BN. LONDON REGT.
(LONDON RIFLE BRIGADE)

2/5. London Rgt.   174/3-8

Sep¹ 1917

23 Div

68
69 } Bdes
70

WAR DIARY 1/2/5 LONDON REGT LRB

INTELLIGENCE SUMMARY

Army Form C. 2118.

(Erase heading not required.)

Hour, Date, Place	Summary of Events and Information	Remarks and references to Appendices
REIGERSBURG Sep 1. 1917	Bn in reserve, training and resting Nil	
5	Maj. R.E. Hill - Williams left Bn to take command of 1/7 Argyle and Sutherland Highlanders RE	
ST JULIEN 8	Bn moved at night into the line N of ST JULIEN relieving the 2/8 Bn. Dispositions A+B Coys in line C in support on STEENBEEK, D in reserve Bn HQ, ALBERTA. Casualties 2/Lt Mivins wounded, 1 O.R. killed 5 O.R. wounded. RE	Ref map POELCAPELLE 1/10000
9	Situation quiet except for occasional heavy shelling of STEENBEEK Mon Du 14, 1BOU and ALBERTA. Two patrols reconnoitred in front of our position no enemy encountered. Casualties 2/Lt Highgate wounded 6 O.R. killed 11 wounded RE	
10	Officer patrols examined enemy wire and reported in fairly good condition. Other patrols reconnoitred advanced enemy positions at C6d 6535 and found them abandoned. Casualties 2 O.R. killed. Capt Palmer RAMC evacuated sick to base, relieved by Capt Coombey RAMC	

LIEUT-COLONEL COMMANDING.
2/5th. (City of London) Battn.

WAR DIARY of 2/5 LONDON REGT LRB

Army Form C. 2118.

INTELLIGENCE SUMMARY.

(Erase heading not required.)

Instructions regarding War Diaries and Intelligence Summaries are contained in F.S. Regs., Part II and the Staff Manual respectively. Title pages will be prepared in manuscript.

Hour, Date, Place		Summary of Events and Information	Remarks and references to Appendices
	1917		
ST JULIEN	Sep. 11	On return of enemy having been seen on derelict tank C.C.24.5.10, (nightly patrols of officers and 20 o.r. went out but no enemy encountered. Casualties 7 o.r. wounded. R.E.	
	12	Bn relieved at night by 2/7 London moved to dugout on CANAL BANK. Casualties 3 o.r. wounded. R.E.	
DAMBRE	13	Move to DAMBRE CAMP about 1 mile N.E. of VLAMERTINGHE. R.E.	
	14	Commenced training for Marine operations. 2/4 Londons returned from feint on Cayenne XVIII Corps attack. R.E.	
	15	Training. R.E.	
	16	Brigade headed for forthcoming attack. R.E.	
	17	do. do.	
	18	do. in evening moved to camp at REIGERSBURG. R.E.	

[signature]
LIEUT.-COLONEL,
COMMANDING.
2/5th (City of London Battⁿ.
LONDON RIFLE BRIGADE

Army Form C. 2118.

WAR DIARY of 2/5 LONDON REGT
or L.R.B.
INTELLIGENCE SUMMARY.

(Erase heading not required.)

Hour, Date, Place	Summary of Events and Information	Remarks and references to Appendices
1917		
REIGERSBURG. Sep 19	"Y" day. The Bn, after having their mid-day meal, paraded late in the afternoon, after a hot meal the Bn paraded late 8 p.m. at 10.45 p.m. to move up to the assembly positions for attack. NE	
ST. JULIEN 20	Zero hour 5.40 a.m. See attached report on operations. The dispositions were 'C' Coy on right 'A' in centre 'D' on left, with 'B' in support. Pontus, Mon Du Hibou, all objectives were taken and consolidated. Many prisoners were taken and captured NE	Appendix "A" attached
21	See attack on 'A'. Notice enemies during the operations:— Killed, Capts B. Furze + G. Whitelaw, 2nd Lts Mitchell, Sherman, Owen, Ward, Dickman, Dennis. Wounded 2nd Lts Green and Loveland. Other Ranks 52 killed 162 wounded 25 missing. Bn relieved on night 21/22 by 2/10 Y London turned out to REIGERSBURG. NE	

/W .... Major
/W .... Lieut-Colonel
COMMANDING.
2nd Bn (City of London) Battn.

Army Form C. 2118.

WAR DIARY
or
INTELLIGENCE SUMMARY.
(Erase heading not required.)

Instructions regarding War Diaries and Intelligence Summaries are contained in F. S. Regs., Part II. and the Staff Manual respectively. Title pages will be prepared in manuscript.

Hour, Date, Place		Summary of Events and Information	Remarks and references to Appendices
	1917		
REIGERSBURG	Sep 22.	Resting. 2/1st Honourable proceeded to Casino on Scheme LETOUQUET Rf.	
BRAKE CAMP	23	Move to BRAKE CAMP A 30 central (Sheet 28 N.W.) 2/1st Brown return from XVIII Corps School Rf.	
	24	Pm resting and refitting. Sergt Conway L.E. & Cpl Price R.G. and Rfn Boston 24th awarded M.M. for gallantry on previous tour in line Sep 10 & Rf.	
	25	Refitting continues. Surplus battle personnel returned from Divi. Nelson Bn together with draft of 3 Officers (2 Lts Piggott, Kenilworth and Howe) and 141 other ranks Rf.	
	26	Reorganizing and training Rf.	
	27	Bn entrained at BRIELEN for AUDRICQ, thence by march route to billets in LICQUES, HERBINGHEM, CAHEN and CANCHY, arriving 10.30 pm. Lt. Col P.D. Stewart proceeded on leave Rf.	

W.——
Lieut-Colonel M.V./n
COMMANDING.
2/5th City of London Battn.
— BRIGADE RIFLE BRIGADE

1/5 London Regt
L.R.B.

WAR DIARY
INTELLIGENCE SUMMARY
Army Form C. 2118

(Erase heading not required.)

Hour, Date, Place	Summary of Events and Information	Remarks and references to Appendices
LICQUES Sep 28 1917	Training	
29	do. Capt J.L. Otter proceeded on leave	
30	Major C.R. Johnston reported from Senior Officers Course ALDERSHOT	

[signature]
for LIEUT-COLONEL,
COMMANDING.
2/5th Bn. City of London Battn.
LONDON RIFLE BRIGADE

REPORT ON OPERATIONS
20/9/17
By
2/5th BATTN. LONDON REGIMENT
(L.R.B)

Appendix "A"

MARCH TO POSITION OF ASSEMBLY.

Battalion paraded ready to march off at 10.45 p.m. on 19th Sept.1917, at REIGERSBURG CAMP, strength 16 Officers and 452 Other Ranks.

The night was very dark, and heavy rain fell from 10 p.m. till about 1 a.m. making the going difficult and slippery.

The Northern duckboard track which ends close to Kitchener's Wood was followed as ordered, and from this point a line across country, the road being obliterated, to BORGHMASTEL, ADAMS FARM, REGINA CROSS ROADS, to HIBOU. This last mile or so was very hard on the men, the leading Company arriving there at 3.40 a.m., and at once formed up on the tape.

POSITION OF ASSEMBLY.

The whole Battalion was in position at about 4.5 a.m., men very tired, fell asleep immediately and were not roused until about 5.20 a.m., when they ate a sandwich ration, with which each man was provided.

There were 4 casualties on the march up, and two wounded on the tape, otherwise the enemy shelling was rather below normal.

ZERO HOUR.

At Zero hour, 5.40 a.m., the whole rose up and advanced in good formation, the flanks of each Company marching on a compass bearing.

ENEMY BARRAGE.

The enemy barrage came down on the usual lines about 4 or 5 minutes after Zero but was not particularly heavy; it kept on thickening, however, until about 6.45 a.m. when it seemed to reach its greatest intensity. This was maintained until after 11 a.m. and at this hour it was concentrated approximately along the line ARBRE - MARINE VIEW - PROMENADE - HUBNER FARM - with a good sprinkling all over the area between this and TIRPITZ - STROPPE FARMS.

DIRECTION.

Much difficulty was experienced in keeping direction owing to the losses among Officers, and the confusing nature of the country. There appeared to be Mebus in every direction - TIRPITZ FARM was only distinguishable by the hedges and ditches around it, and in the same way STROPPE and GENOA could only be guessed at. It appears that the direction generally was rather too much to the left, but this was recognised and the right Company of the Battalion swung round and struck DIMPLE TRENCH and ARBRE.

CASUALTIES.

"A" and "B" Companies' casualties occurred chiefly before reaching HUBNER TRENCH, "A" Coy. losing all 3 Officers, and "B" Coy. 2 Officers. More casualties were suffered around HUBNER FARM and the Mebus just West of it. Here the leading troops were held up and "D" and "A" Coys. went forward and came under heavy Machine Gun fire.

Some of the 51st Division participated in the attack on HUBNER FARM believing it to be QUEBEC FARM.

BARRAGE.

Our own barrage was very intense and all agree that very heavy casualties were inflicted on the enemy during his counter-attacks.

As was to be expected a few casualties were suffered by our men, but the number was small.

MACHINE GUNS.

Enemy's machine guns were very active from our right in HUBNER TRENCH and later from positions in shell-holes and shelters at HUBNER FARM and in DIMPLE TRENCH.

Our machine guns were up with the front line throughout, and the Section Officer on our left actually took charge of his portion of the line.

Our overhead machine gun barrage could be heard throughout, but there is no means of telling how effective it proved.

(1)

COMMUNICATIONS.

After the objective was reached, the approximate position of the front line was reported back by means of "message maps". The fact that so many Officers and Company Runners became casualties in the early stages, made it very difficult to get information back from the front line.

CONSOLIDATION.

All the men available at the finish of the advance, consolidated a shell-hole position running in an irregular line roughly through D 1 Central, D 1 d 14, D 7 a 6.8, with forward posts at STROPPE and TIRPITZ FARMS, a small party being kept in support in the neighbourhood of D 1 c 62. The posts at STROPPE and TIRPITZ FARMS were then relieved by platoons of "B" Coy. of 2/7th Battn. London Regt., who consolidated strong posts at each place.

COUNTER-ATTACKS.

During the afternoon of the 20th., small parties of the enemy were observed moving about in the neighbourhood of WINCHESTER FARM and on the ridge in the distance. At about 6 p.m. it became evident that the enemy were going to make a counter-attack. They advanced in small bodies, but when the leading bodies had approached to within about 1,000 yards of our line, our Artillery put down a very heavy barrage and our Machine Guns opened fire with the result that the enemy were cut to pieces and could be seen running away.

Just before dawn on 21st September, our Artillery put down another heavy barrage, but it was not apparent that any enemy counter-attack ever started. On the evening of the 21st., the enemy again made a counter-attack, their Infantry advancing by twos and threes for some considerable time previously. The barrage was repeated with the same result. During each counter-attack the enemy put down a barrage of heavy shells on the line GENOA - HUBNER, and behind. This barrage moved back and forward and was particularly heavy on the second evening.

TOTAL CASUALTIES.

      9 Officers killed.
      3 Officers wounded.
      44 Other Ranks killed. (52)
      156 Other Ranks wounded. (162)
      39 Other Ranks missing. (25)

There were 11 Lewis Guns brought back, 3 of which were damaged.

SECRET.

Appendix 12

OPERATION ORDER NO. 23

Copy No. 10.
26/9/17.

2/6th Bn. THE LONDON REGIMENT.

1. The Battalion will move to the new area tomorrow, 27/9/17.

2. Companies will parade at 8.15 a.m. and march off in the following order:

        A. Coy.
        B. Coy.
        C. Coy.
        D. Coy.

at 200 yards distance.

3. Leading Company will pass starting point (point in sleeper track 200 yards S.E. of cross-roads at A.30.d.19.) at 8.45 a.m. following the 5th Battalion.

4. Paradex States shewing exact number entraining will be rendered to Battalion Orderly Room at 7.45 a.m. and a note of the actual numbers on parade will be handed to the Assistant Adjutant at starting point. 2/Lieut. A.H. TEW will furnish parade state for Headquarters and note of actual numbers.

5. ROUTE. SLEEPER track W. of VLAMERTINGHE and VLAMERTINGHE - BRIELEN ROAD.

6. The Battalion will arrive at BRIELEN station at 10 a.m. and leave by first train at 11.30 a.m. Capt. H.H. BROWNE will act as entraining officer. Brigade entraining officer is Lieut. HARRISON-JONES.

7. Battalion will detrain at AUDRUICQ and march to billets at AUDENFORT.

8. DRESS. Full marching order with helmets.
Packs will be dumped on arrival at AUDRUICQ station under a guard furnished by A.Coy. whence they will be carried by lorry to destination.

9. LEWIS GUNS. will be carried to BRIELEN. Lewis Gun magazines will be taken by limber. Guns and magazines will be stacked in covered vans on the train. The Lewis Gun Officer will be responsible for loading magazines into limber and into covered wagons.

10. WATER. Water bottles will be filled immediately after breakfast before leaving camp and the water will not be used without orders.

11. TOMMY COOKERS. A supply has been issued to Companies for heating food on the journey. These are not to be used until ordered.

12. RATIONS. Unexpended portion of the day's rations will be carried. Rations for the 28th will be issued in the new area.

13. MESS CART. Mess boxes to be ready packed and stacked outside Mess at 8 a.m.

14. DISCIPLINE. No man will leave the train without permission. A.C. & D. Coys. will furnish picquets at all stops to see that these orders are enforced.

15. ACKNOWLEDGE.

Signed:- S.W.F. Crofts, 2/Lieut
Acting Adjutant, 2/6th Bn. The London Regt.

WAR DIARY
INTELLIGENCE SUMMARY

of 2/5 Bn London Regt Army Form C. 2118.
L.R.B.

Hour, Date, Place	Summary of Events and Information	Remarks and references to Appendices
Oct 1917 LICQUES	Training	
2	2/Lt L.G. Hammerline returns from G.H.Q. Lewis Gun School VI.	
6	2/Lt W. Grove (13 finishes) reported for duty on first appointment	
	MILITARY MEDAL awarded to 25 other ranks of the Battn. for the operation of 20/21 Septr. 2/Lt A.C. Juno returns from duty in Corps Mountain School. Capt. C. Judge returns from France Depot VI.	
8	Capt 2/Lt. Otter returns from leave UK.	
10	2/Lt 2/R Reeve returns from Convalescent camp BOULOGNE VI. Further awards for the operation of 20/21 Septr as under: D.S.O. — Lt.Col. P.D. Stewart M.C. Capt 2/Lt. Otter D.C.M. 6 other ranks M.M. 1 other rank	
11	Lt. Col. P.D. Stewart D.S.O. returns from leave and took on temporary command of ⅔ Bde in the absence of Brig. Gen. G. Higgins D.S.O.	
12	2/Lt G.R. Reeve proceeded on leave to England 2/Lt J. Wilkinson to 19 Corps School (Lewis Gun) VI. Capt C. Judge to 18 Corps Reinforcement Camp VI.	

WAR DIARY of 2/5 Bn London Regt
LRB
Army Form C. 2118.

INTELLIGENCE SUMMARY

Hour, Date, Place	Summary of Events and Information	Remarks and references to Appendices
1917		
Oct. 15 LICQUES	2/Lts LHGillus MRS, Wright (18th London) and T.A. Howell reported for duty. G 151 appointment RC	
19	Orders received for move to [proceed] area RC	
20 POPERINGHE	Bn moved by train to POPERINGHE, arriving in the town [tow?] are PD Stewart DSO arrived in the town & ??? PD Stewart DSO resumed command of the Bn. RC	
24 SEIGE CAMP	Moved from POPERINGHE to SEIGE CAMP (about 2 mile N of VLAMERTINGHE) Capt J.Otto MC and midday. Little personnel proceeded to Dine Depôt from HOUTKERQUE 2/Lt Attwaters reports for duty at Depôt Bn. RC	Ref. Map ST JULIEN 28 N.W.
25	receiving and preparation for attack RC	
26 CANAL BANK	Orders received at 2.30 p.m. to move during the afternoon. Bn marched out at 4 p.m. to Augustown CANAL BANK RC	
27	Bn in working parties in the forward area RC 20 o.r. wounded	
28	Working parties. Casualties 10 o.r. wounded. Orders received to move in the morning of the 29a night late in the day when [orders] moved to KEMPTON PARK & [bivouacked] into the lines to KEMPTON PARK in the night of 29a and [orders] at ????? to [Assembly] attack [position] in the morning of the 30a during our attack [order?] by the 6 + 8 Bn, RC	P.D. Stewart

(73989) W4141-463. 400,000. 9/14. H.&J.Ltd. Forms/C. 2118/10.

WAR DIARY 1/7th Bn London Regt

INTELLIGENCE SUMMARY

Army Form C. 2118.

Hour, Date, Place	Summary of Events and Information	Remarks and references to Appendices
1917		
29 KEMPTON PARK	Moved to KEMPTON PARK in the evening and rested the night in minen huts. 2/Lts. J. Piggott and R.W.C. Nace rejoined from 1st Corps School. Casualties 1 O.R. wounded N.Y.	
30 POELCAPELLE	At 5.50 a.m. (Zero hour) Bn. moved to PHEASANT FM when Coy. was disposed in shellholes in its rear. TRENCH area. Weather very wet throughout during day. At 5 p.m. unless orders to take over the line from the 6 Regt Bn afternoon attack and to send any active patrols to clean no situation which was not clear. Relief [unclear] to distribution being "B" Coy on right in TRACAS FARM area, "A" Coy on left (Baton.) "C" in HELLES HOUSE, "D" Coy in support, one Coy J. Bn (under orders of 5 Bn) in reserve at PHEASANT TRENCH Posts occupied that MORAY HOUSE, HINTON FM PAPA FM and CAMERON HOUSE were also held. Casualties 2/Lt R.P. Kenthwaite wounded 3 O.R. killed 20 wounded N.Y.	Ref. Map. POELCAPELLE Sheet 1/10000

WAR DIARY of 2/5 Bn London Regt LRB

INTELLIGENCE SUMMARY

Hour, Date, Place	Summary of Events and Information	Remarks and references to Appendices
Oct 31 1917 POELCAPELLE	'A' Coy having been ordered to think in their effort how to get close touch with enemy 'D' which was found in front of an enemy line on about V 20 b 40 80. It was decided to attack this from "D" Coy being ordered to make the attack not 'A' Coy cooperating in support, one platoon of "D" under 2/Lt Stone moved on 5 Pm from their right from and attacked from a N.E. direction. The guns were had ammunition. Moving forward extremely strong opposition from difficulty. They met with heavy machine gun in a line of [shell holes] E and S.] the objective and suffered a number of casualties including 2/Lt Stone who was wounded, a few part from the position were rather men reached the line and pieces 3 awaiting his return withdrew a platoon of 'A' Coy under 3/ again to the party awaiting was driven off by to mine E along the SPRIET Road, was heavy barrage which came down on the road. Patrols was unable to take part in the attack after the and no to locate the wounded were attack whenever that the enemy were remainder were holding strongly hel[d].	Ref Map POELCAPELLE Sheet 1/6000 D.F. Spence

(CONTD.)

Army Form C. 2118.

WAR DIARY
or
INTELLIGENCE SUMMARY.
(Erase heading not required.)

Instructions regarding War Diaries and Intelligence Summaries are contained in F.S. Regs., Part II and the Staff Manual respectively. Title pages will be prepared in manuscript.

Hour, Date, Place	Summary of Events and Information	Remarks and references to Appendices
1917 Oct. 31 POELCAPELLE (cont'd)	The Bn was relieved in the line at night by the 2/9" London Regt and moved back to KEMPTON PARK moving from there by lorries to SEIGE CAMP Casualties 2/Lt RH STOREY wounded and missing 8 O.R. killed 10 o.r. wounded 1 o.r. wounded and missing 4 o.r. missing	[signature]

WAR DIARY of 2/5 London Regt LRB
INTELLIGENCE SUMMARY

Army Form C. 2118.

Place	Hour, Date	Summary of Events and Information	Remarks and references to Appendices
SIEGE CAMP	Nov. 1 1917	Relief from line carried out in early morning. Bn. resting all day. R/.	
	2	Refitting and resting. Revr in same billets R/.	
	3	New R.C. James C.F. reported for duty in place of Williamson returned from XIV Corps School R/.	
	4	3 offrs & 200 o.r. under Capt. R.C. Kitching proceeded to GWENT FARM for attachment to RAMC for stretcher bearing work in forward area. 100 o.r. on working party in line. Casualties 2 o.r. killed R/.	
	6	Reinforcing draft of 84 o.r. joined from Depot Bn. R/.	
	7	Orders received for move forward. Preparations to execute R/. attachment to V. army sniping school R/.	
	8	Bn. moved to dugouts in CANAL BANK. Lt Col P.D. Stewart in 4 days sick leave. Maj. C.E. Goventin assumed command. Capt. Kitching & 7 offrs & 300 o.r. rejoined from attachment to RAMC R/.	
CANAL BANK	10	Bn. moved up into support at KEMPTON PARK and A Coy in forward position at PHEASANT TRENCH under the orders of O.C. Rath in line R/.	
KEMPTON PARK	11	'A' Coy relieved in PHEASANT TRENCH by 'D' Coy. Casualties 1 o.r. killed 1 o.r. wounded R/.	

J.R. Somerton Mjr
for LIEUT.-COLONEL, COMMANDING.
2/5th. (City of London) Battn.
LONDON RIFLE BRIGADE.

WAR DIARY of 2/5 London Regt LRB
INTELLIGENCE SUMMARY

Army Form C. 2118.

Hour, Date, Place	Summary of Events and Information	Remarks and references to Appendices
KEMPTON PARK Nov. 12 1917	Bn relieved 2/6 Bn in line on night 12/13. Casualties during relief 3 O.R. wounded. Dispositions:- Bn HQ. NORFOLK HOUSE. 'B' Coy in right in TRACAS FM area. 'A' Coy centre MEUNIER HQ. area. 'C' Coy left NOBLES FM area. 'D' Coy in support with HQ. and 1 platoon at BREWERY, 1 platoon GLOSTER FM. Reserve coy 2/6 1/1 London in PHEASANT TRENCH. Owing to low strength of Batt. platoons were amalgamated so as to give each Coy 2 strong platoon each and 2 fewer in reserve. When in line were made up:- 'A'. 'B'. 'C'. 'D'. H.Q. Major C.S. Johnston (Cmdg) Capt E.C. Moore 2/Lt Godmond Capt Welchman Capt R.Cope (adjt) 2/Lt Jones - Jones 2/Lt Hummerstone 2/Lt G.R. Reeve 2/Lt Puggot - Ware - Hewens - Morris (Int Offr) (C.Coy) 2/Lt Jw Carrington (Signals) Capt H.S. Palmer R.A.M.C. 2 Main Batteries went out on relief N.R.	Ref. Map SPRIET 1/10000
POELCAPELLE 13	Quiet day. Casualties nil N.R.	

LIEUT.-COLONEL, COMMANDING.
2/5th. (City of London) Batt:
LONDON RIFLE BRIGADE

Army Form C. 2118.

WAR DIARY of 2/5 London LRB
INTELLIGENCE SUMMARY
(Erase heading not required.)

Instructions regarding War Diaries and Intelligence Summaries are contained in F.S. Regs., Part II and the Staff Manual respectively. Title pages will be prepared in manuscript.

Hour, Date, Place		Summary of Events and Information	Remarks and references to Appendices
POELCAPELLE	Nov. 14 1917	Disposition settled in morning. Companies by 6 a.m. as under:— Support Coy H.Q. and 'C' Coy to Helwen Shelters in POELCAPELLE. Left Coy H.Q. and local support to BREWERY. Centre Coy H.Q. and local support to POELCAPELLE. Relieve some nights by 2/1 Londons and move to KEMPTON PARK less 'D' Coy who move to support positions at PHEASANT TRENCH under orders of O.C. 2/1 Bn. Casualties 1 o.r. killed. V.C.	
KEMPTON PARK	15	Move to CANAL BANK and reported by 'D' Coy. V.C.	
CANAL BANK	16	Move to SIEGE CAMP. M.Col. P.D. Stewart D.S.O. reports from sick leave. 2/Lt Sandham Wykeham on leave. V.C.	
SIEGE CAMP	17	Move by train to HERZEELE and surrounding farms and billets in village (1st London Regt. atto) reports 1/5 Bower and Crook 2/Lts Brown reports for duty. V.C.	
HERZEELE	18	Bn. resting and refitting. 2/Lt a.e. Young rejoins from duties as Town Major REIGERSBURG CAMP. V.C.	
	19	morning V.C.	
	20		
	21		
	22		
	23		

[signature] Major
LIEUT.—COLONEL,
COMMANDING.
2/5th. (City of London) Battn.
LONDON RIFLE BRIGADE.

Army Form C. 2118.

WAR DIARY of 2/5th London Regt.
L.R.B.

INTELLIGENCE SUMMARY.

(Erase heading not required.)

Instructions regarding War Diaries and Intelligence Summaries are contained in F.S. Regs., Part II and the Staff Manual respectively. Title pages will be prepared in manuscript.

Hour, Date, Place 1917		Summary of Events and Information	Remarks and references to Appendices
HERZEELE	Nov. 24	2/5 J.S. Andrews to V Corps Instructor Camp. Orders received for move to new area.	RC.
	25	Bn. (less transport) moved by march route to PIGEON CAMP, PROVEN. Transport moved to new area by night.	Ref. sheet. HAZEBROUCK 1/100000
PROVEN	26	Moved by train from PROVEN to WIZERNE, thence 9 miles to SENINGHEM, rejoining by transport and billeted for night.	
SENINGHEM	27	Moved by march route to LOTTINGHEM.	RC.
LOTTINGHEM	28	Lt. Col. P.D. Stewart D.S.O. to XVIII Corps conference BOLLEZEELE.	Ref. sheet. CALAIS 1/100000
	29	Bn. training	RC.
	30	do	RC.

Atherton Major
for LIEUT.-COLONEL
COMMANDING.
2/5th (City of London) Battn.
LONDON RIFLE BRIGADE.

WAR DIARY of 2/5 London Regt LRB

Army Form C. 2118.

INTELLIGENCE SUMMARY

(Erase heading not required.)

Instructions regarding War Diaries and Intelligence Summaries are contained in F.S. Regs., Part II and the Staff Manual respectively. Title pages will be prepared in manuscript.

Place	Hour, Date, 1917	Summary of Events and Information	Remarks and references to Appendices
LOTTINGHEM	Dec 1	Training. Lt. Col. P.O. Stewart DSO. returned from Senior Officers Training Conference. N.C.	Ref. Map CALAIS 1/100000
	2	2/Lts A.C. Jones & S. Hunterstone to II Corps Infantry School. 2/Lt F. Smethurst returned from gunnery course. N.C.	
	4	Capt J.E. Otter proceeded to duty at 58th Divl H.Q. N.C.	
	6	Orders received that the Division were now to be found were a sector of the line by the 10th inst. This Battn. moving in its pre-commencing stations its training leave, which had been somewhat interrupted by various moves. It is being at HERZEELE and LOTTINGHEM however enabled the draft reserve coming however absorbed in the Battalion & receive its instruction to keep bomb throwing and rifle grenadier and live ammunition in these sections. N.C.	
	7	Marched to COULOMBY and billets (no transfer N.C.	P Stewart Lt Col. Ref. Map HAZEBROUCK 1/100000

Army Form C. 2118.

WAR DIARY of 2/5 London Regt
LRB
INTELLIGENCE SUMMARY.

(Erase heading not required.)

Instructions regarding War Diaries and Intelligence Summaries are contained in F.S. Regs., Part II and the Staff Manual respectively. Title pages will be prepared in manuscript.

Hour, Date, Place		Summary of Events and Information	Remarks and references to Appendices
COULOMBY	Dec. 8 1917	Marched 11 miles to WIZERNES, entrained & proceeded to ELVERDINGHE. From Ry. head marched to "F" CAMP A.15.c, arriving about 3 am 9th inst.	Ry/head, BELGIUM 28 N.W.
'F' CAMP	9	Marched to DIRTY BUCKET CAMP	
DIRTY BUCKET	10	Orders received that the 174th Bde were remaining in reserve during the forthcoming Divisional Tour in the line and were proceeding into winter huts for the Division while the 173 & 175 Brigades held the line. This Bn. to move to HUDDLESTONE CAMP C.17.d.34 and remain there during the tour.	
	11	2/Lt. D. Paggett and ratting platoon of 30 o.r. left for attachment to 504th Field Coy R.E.	
	12	Marched to HUDDLESTONE CAMP. H.Q. and 2 Coys in Nissen huts, 2 Coys in sandbagged dugouts.	
HUDDLESTONE CAMP	13	Whole Battalion on work in camp, improving huts and dugouts &c.	P. Stewart Lt/Col.
	14	Commenced running parties for R.E. Tunnelling Coy and R.F.A.	

WAR DIARY of 2/5 London Regt. Army Form C. 2118.
or
INTELLIGENCE SUMMARY.   L.R.B.
(Erase heading not required.)

Hour, Date, Place	Summary of Events and Information	Remarks and references to Appendices
HUDDLESTONE CAMP Dec. 15 1917	Working parties. 5 sergeants 2/Lt Gythwin to 5th Army infantry School. RE	
16	2/Lt Graham returned from 5th Army Infantry School on command of B Coy, vice Capt. 2/Lt Otto, W.Coe. P.D. Stewart D.S.O. to Paris on leave. Major C.E. Johnston taking command. Completed in working parties. 20 o.r. killed, 3 wounded. RE	
17–18	Working parties. RE.	
19	Mr Gridwood ammu cutting rank & Captain while in command of a Coy, receiving Sergeants notice. RE.	
20	W. Bell, 102 U.S.A. Infantry arrived for instruction. RE 1/R 48 from attachment.	
22	R. Bell ceased to be attached. Completed 2/Lt. Brown missing is could from a M.G. bullet believed to have been from an enemy aircraft. 4 o.r. wounded on working parties. RE	P.S. Stewart Capt.

WAR DIARY or INTELLIGENCE SUMMARY.

(Erase heading not required.)

Army Form C. 2118.

WAR DIARY of 2/5 London Regt. L.R.B.

Hour, Date, Place	Summary of Events and Information	Remarks and references to Appendices
HUDDLESTONE CAMP 1917 Dec. 23	Working parties. Lt.Col. P.D. Stewart D.S.O. returned from Paris and assumed command of 174th Bde in the absence of Brig. Gen. Higgins D.S.O. W.C.	
25	Working parties. W.C.	
27	Capt. G.C. Kitching proceeded on leave to England W.C.	

28	Majors & 7 Officers arrived companies:
	 Majors S. Powers — to 'A' Coy
	        E.V. Jr. Fegg — " 'D' "
	        V.A. Dudoyen — " A "
	 2nd Lt. C. Hare — " C "
	 2nd Lt. H.C. Fulton — " B "
	 C.S.M. Brodie — " C "
	 H.L. Higgs — " A " W.C.	

30	Lt.Col. P.D. Stewart D.S.O. resumed command. W.C.	P.D. Stewart Lt.Col.

31	Working parties. Strength of Bn at beginning of month was 928 to Coy. 835 ration. as end of month 899 total 625 ration. Difference in ration strength been due to 90 men details
	     " " 10 " on course
	     " " 50 " " leave
	     " " 25 " sick
	 W.C.	

WAR DIARY
or
INTELLIGENCE SUMMARY.
(Erase heading not required.)

Army Form C. 2118.

2/5 London R

Hour, Date, Place	Summary of Events and Information	Remarks and references to Appendices
HUDDLESTON CAMP, JAN 1st	Whole Battalion was on working parties in the PILCKEM – LANGEMARCK area, until Jan 8th. SRR	
	2nd Revd. H.C. JAMES C.F. proceeded to Chaplains School, ST. OMER. SRR	
	Col. P.D. STEWART & Capt. E.G. MOORE proceeded to duty with 58th Divisional Depot Battalion. SRR	
	3rd Major C.E. JOHNSTON assumed command of the Battalion. SRR	
	Capt H.G. WILKINSON proceeded to R.E. Centre, G.H.Q. S.A. School LE TOUQUET SRR	
	2/Lt. R. BRONNER proceeded on 6 days leave to PARIS. SRR	
	4th 2/Lts. L.G. HUMMERSTONE & A.L. JONES returned from duty from II Corps Infantry School. SRR	
	5th 2/Lt. A.C. YOUNG returned from II Corps Sch. the Bourse. SRR	
	2/Lt. R.S.S. WRIGHT returned from duty with 175th Sew Savage Coy. SRR	
	2/Lt. A.M.C. HALL attached to Tremont Section SRR.	
	7th 2/Lt. J. PIGGOTT & Sapping Parton returned to duty from attachment to South British Coy R.E. SRR	
	2. O.R's wounded in action. SRR	
ROAD CAMP, PROVEN (ST JAN-TER-BIEZEN)	8th Battalion moved to ROAD CAMP, PROVEN (St JAN-TER-BIETZEN) P. Coming BOSINGHE 10.30am. Remained PROVEN 1:30am & marched to ROAD CAMP – Men carried out during & after snowstorm. SRR	
	One Platoon under Lt. C. HALL remained at duty with the 153rd Tunnelling Coy. on forward area rejoining the Battalion at ROAD CAMP the following day. SRR	
	Rev. F. WILLIAMSON proceeded to England on leave SRR	
	9/10 J.H. MORRIS rejoined from 58th Divisional School SRR	

2/5TH (CITY OF LONDON) BATTALION
LONDON BRIGADE.

Army Form C. 2118.

WAR DIARY
or
INTELLIGENCE SUMMARY.
(Erase heading not required.)

Instructions regarding War Diaries and Intelligence Summaries are contained in F.S. Regs., Part II. and the Staff Manual respectively. Title pages will be prepared in manuscript.

Hour, Date, Place	Summary of Events and Information	Remarks and references to Appendices
ROAD CAMP, PROVEN, JAN 9th (ST JAN-TER-BIESTEN)	Day devoted to checking of deficiencies, reorganisation of Coys. & cleaning. LRB	
	Lt. R.F. LYDALL, 2/Lt. R.E. PETLEY M.C., H.J.F. CRISP, joined for duty. LRB. Gazette notice received Lt (a/Capt) H.G. WILKINSON, to be Capt. 11/6/17 (London Gazette 5th Supplement D/- 21/12/17) LRB	
10th	Training. Range Practices. Aircraft Cover Bombing. LRB	
(crossed out)	Lt.Col. P.D. STEWART D.S.O returned from duty with 5th Div Depot Bn, & assumed command of 174th Inf Bde during absence of Brigadier General C.G. HIGGINS D.S.O LRB	
	Rev. H.C. JAMES C.F. returned from Chaplains School ST. OMER. LRB.	
11th	Lt A.H. CROOK proceeded to England to report M.G. Centre GRANTHAM. LRB	
12th	G.O.C. II Corps, Sir CLAUDE JACOB, K.C.B presented medal ribands for awards of decorations to 173rd & 174th Inf. Bdes, the following of the battalion were recipients:
Lt. KENT. M.J., Military Cross,
Lt. LINTOTT. A.T.C Military Cross,
19 O.R's, Military Medal LRB
3 O.R's, B.C.M	
13th	2/Lt R. BRONNER returned from Para-leave School GRA	
14th	2/Lt. B.R. POTTER proceeded to I Corps Anti Gas School GRA	
15th	2/Lt R. BRONNER proceeded to R.9 Course at G.H.Q. S.A. School LE TOQUET GRA	
15th	Capt. H.G. WILKINSON returned from Lewis Gun Course. GRA	
16th	Lt. C. HALL + 60 O.R's proceeded as advance party to new area. GRA Orders received that the Division was moving South, into army of the Battalion being 19th. GRA	
	2/Lt. H.W. SAMPSON proceeded to I Corps Lewis Gun School GRA	

(signature) Lt.Col. Commanding
2/5TH (CITY OF LONDON) BATTALION
LONDON RIFLE BRIGADE.

WAR DIARY or INTELLIGENCE SUMMARY.

(Erase heading not required.)

Army Form C. 2118.

Instructions regarding War Diaries and Intelligence Summaries are contained in F.S. Regs., Part II and the Staff Manual respectively. Title pages will be prepared in manuscript.

Hour, Date, Place	Summary of Events and Information	Remarks and references to Appendices
ROAD CAMP, PROVEN (ST JAN-TER-ZIETZEN) 17th / 18th	During the occupation of this camp useful training was carried out, particular attention being paid to the following. Physical & Bayonet training, Range practices + Lewis Gun firing, Classes for Runners, Bombers, Lewis Gun + Junior N.C.Os were held. Battalion was practised in lining up in the open, + Tactical schemes for officers were carried out. GRR	
MOREUIL 19th	Battalion moved to 5th Army area – Moved to PROVEN, entraining there at 9.30 am – stopped for 40 minutes at TINQUES for tea, detrained at VILLERS BRETONNEUX where hot soup was obtained by Troops. Battalion then marched to billets at MOREUIL about 8 miles south of V.B. arriving at 4 am. GRR	
20th	Men rested. Returned w/o billets. GRR	
"	2/Lt R.B. POTER rejoined from II Corps Gas School. GRR	
21st	Training commenced. Lewis Gun, Bombing + Signalling Classes. GRR	
22nd	Continuation of training. GRR	
23rd	do. GRR	
24th	Capt + Adjt R. COPE proceeded on leave to England. GCR. Lt Col P.D. STEWART D.S.O. assumed the duties vacated i/c of Hon proceeded to G.H.Q. S.A. School CAMIERS preparatory to taking command of 58th Bn N/G Battalion. GCR	
25th	Capt. G.C. KITCHING + 2/Lt F. WILLIAMSON rejoined from leave. GCR	
26th	Continuation of training. Tactical School for officers by G.O.C. Division. GCR	

2/5TH BN LONDON BATTALION
LONDON RIFLE BRIGADE

Army Form C. 2118.

WAR DIARY
or
INTELLIGENCE SUMMARY.
(Erase heading not required.)

Instructions regarding War Diaries and Intelligence Summaries are contained in F.S. Regs., Part II and the Staff Manual respectively. Title pages will be prepared in manuscript.

Hour, Date, Place	Summary of Events and Information	Remarks and references to Appendices
MOREUIL Jan 27th.	Training & billeting facilities in this area were excellent & fullest advantage was taken of the opportunity afforded. Orders were received that under D.A.G. letter S/9094 the Battalion was to be disbanded as follows:— 7 Officers + 150 O.Rs to 2/10 London Regiment (Hackney) 10 Officers + 250 O.Rs to 1/18th do. (London Irish) L.R. 18 Officers + 450 O.Rs to 1/28th do. (Artists Rifles) L.R.	
28th.	Day spent in handing in of stores, preparation of inventories & nominal rolls for the disbandment. S.A.A.	
29th.	The party for the 1/28 London Regiment (Artists Rifles):— Capt. FURZE C. " KITCHING G.C. " WILKINSON H.G. " MOORE E.S. Lt. WILLIAMSON F. " LEGG T.F. " PETLEY R.E. M.C. 2/Lt. LINTOTT H.C. " BRODIE C.F.C. " SAMPSON H.W. " HUMMERSTONE L.G. " REEVE G.R. " YOUNG A.C. " GORE W. " PIGGOTT J. " NEWELL F.A. " MORRIS J.H. " HIGGS H.L. & 450 O.Rs ("C" & "D" Coys.) (Less 6 officers marked * & 102 O.Rs who were not immediately available owing to leave, courses, sickness or duty.) Paraded at 8 a.m. in the Square MOREUIL & were addressed by B.G.C. 174th Inf. Bde. who in his address impressed on all ranks that they should at all times maintain the high standard of discipline & efficiency shown whilst serving with the 2nd Battn London Rifle Brigade	

Army Form C. 2118.

WAR DIARY
or
INTELLIGENCE SUMMARY.
(Erase heading not required.)

Hour, Date, Place	Summary of Events and Information	Remarks and references to Appendices
MOREUIL Jan. 29th (contd.)	The party then embussed + proceeded to join their new Battalion GRR.	
	The remainder of the Battalion was formed up on the training ground at 11.30 a.m. + were addressed by G.O.C. 58th Division Major General A.F. Cator D.S.O. who congratulated the Battalion on their achievements in	
30th	Capt. the Adjut. + various other ranks Gros Frech GRR Capt. H.S. PALMER (RAMC) Medical officer received instructions to report to 72nd H.C. Field amb GRR The party for the 1/18th London Regiment (London Irish Rifles):-	
	CAPT GODWARD J.S. Lt HALL C. " LYDALL R.F. " CRISP H.J.F. 2/Lt PILCHER A.M. " WRIGHT R.G.S " JONES A.L. - CARRINGTON J.W. x - BROWNER R. x - HALL R.W.C. & 250 O.R. ("A" coy surplus + B coy) (less 2 officers marked x + 50 O.R. who were not immediately available owing to leave, courses, sickness or duty.)	
	Paraded at 8 a.m. + embussed + proceeded to join their new Regiment GRR.	
BERTEAUCOURT + THENNES	The remainder of Battalion (part of A Coy for 2/10th London Regt + HQ Personnel) moved by march route, with Q.M. Stores + Transport to THENNES - 3 miles north of MOREUIL GRR	
31st	2/Lt L SMETHAM proceeded on leave to England UK The party for the 2/10th London Regiment:-	

Signed [signature]
Major Commanding
21st (County of London) Battalion
LONDON RIFLE BRIGADE

WAR DIARY
or
INTELLIGENCE SUMMARY.
(Erase heading not required.)

Army Form C. 2118.

Hour, Date, Place	Summary of Events and Information	Remarks and references to Appendices

THENNES
Jan 3rd
(contd.)
	MAJOR BOWERS S.
	2/Lt JONES C.H
	* " LINTOTT A.J.C. M.C.
	* " WIMBLE A.S.
	* " FINLAYSON V.A
	2/Lt " POWER B.R.
	* " SMETHAM L.
	
	+ 150 O.Rs ("A" Coy)
	(less 4 officers + 38 O.Rs who were not immediately available owing to leave, course, sickness, duty)
	
	Paraded outside their billet at 10 a.m. + proceeded by march route to join their new battalion at FOUILLOY E.R.R.
	
	After this party had left the surplus men with Battalion consisted of 6 officers + 17 O.Rs HQ Personnel
	  36 O.Rs Transport Reserves after their parties had
	  18 O.Rs left 6 guns + Battalions
	
	The 6 officers were:-
	MAJOR C.E. JOHNSTON Commanding
	REV. H.C. JAMES C.F.
	Lt. H.J. KENT M.C. Q.M.
	Lt. A.J.C. LINTOTT M.C. Transport Officer
	2/Lt. G.R. REEVE acting Adjutant during absence of Capt W
	R. COPE on leave
	2/Lt. R.W.C. HALL Asst Transport Officer
		[signature]
		GCR
		2 Lt. City of London Battalion
		London [illegible] Brigade

	ions	Sent		Service.	
	At.............m.			From.........
	To...............		(Signature of "Franking Officer.")	By............
	By...............			

TO T.O.   Vile

Sender's Number.	Day of Month.	In reply to Number.	AAA
* T/005	17		

Ref letter to 24th
Field Amb Lady is
requested not to
not to interfere with
any War arrangements you
have made

From ZETE
Place
Time 21.00 hrs

The above may be forwarded as now corrected. (2) [signature]
Censor. Signature of Addressor or person authorised to telegraph in his name.
* This line should be erased if not required.

www.ingramcontent.com/pod-product-compliance
Lightning Source LLC
Chambersburg PA
CBHW081454160426
43193CB00013B/2475